Climbing

Written by
Jill Atkins

Climbing is a cool activity for children and adults.

Little children like to climb on a climbing frame. They may have one in their garden, at nursery or at school.

It might have a ladder, a slide or a swing.

These children are playing in a tree house.

They can climb up a ladder to get into it. They can pretend it is their home.

You can go to the park, too, where there might be lots of things to clamber on.

Rope ladders and nets are fun, but you need strong arms and legs to hang on!

This girl must have really strong limbs!

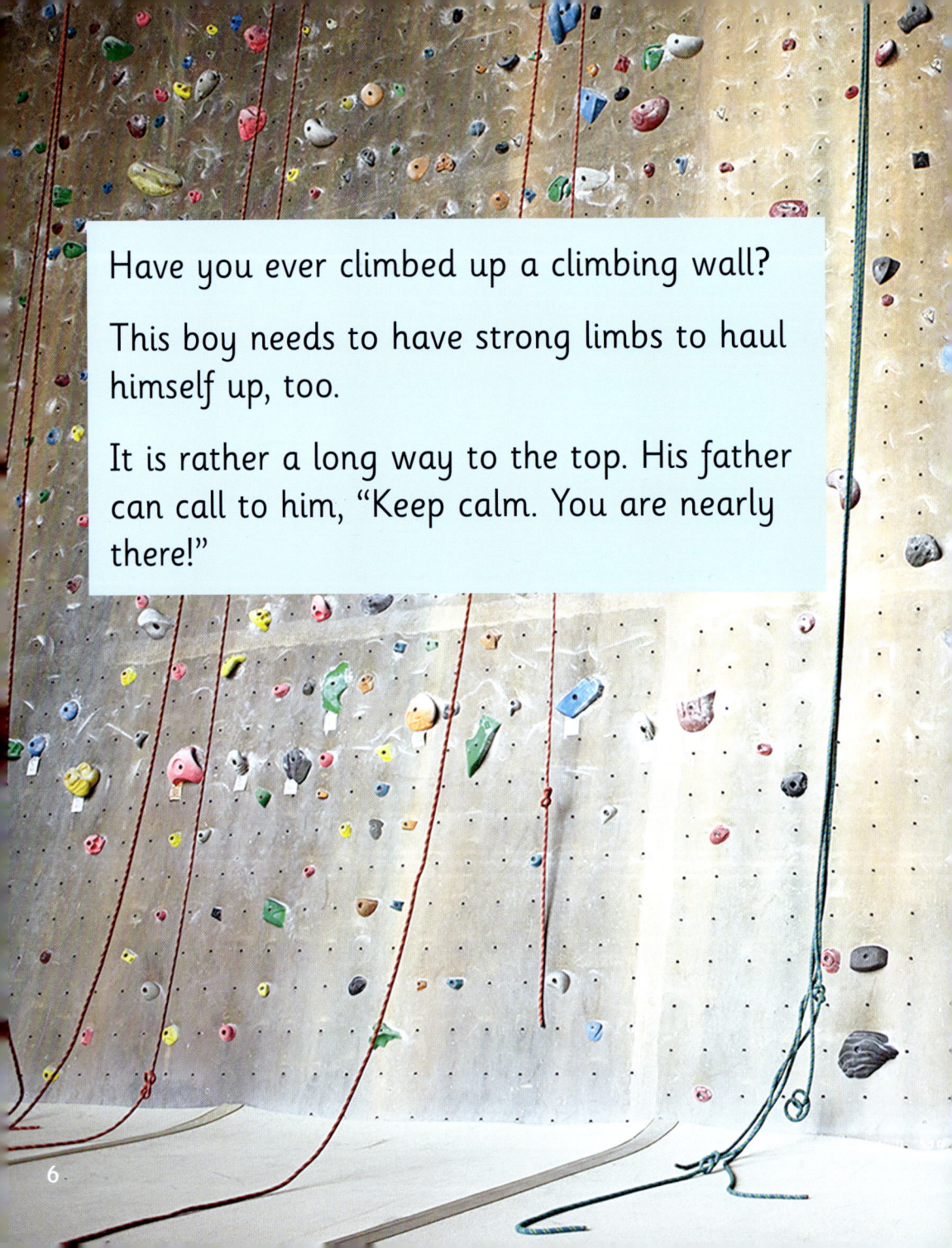

Have you ever climbed up a climbing wall?

This boy needs to have strong limbs to haul himself up, too.

It is rather a long way to the top. His father can call to him, "Keep calm. You are nearly there!"

People can climb in lots of places in town or in the wild.

This man is getting down from the coconut palm tree he has just climbed. He has picked some coconuts from the tree.

These children are climbing a tree too, but there are no coconuts in this tree!

You can climb steps or stairs, but sometimes they can be rather steep.

If they are steep, some people like to have a handrail to help them up — and to stop them falling down.

If you go up a steep path, you can have a rest on the grass when you reach the top of the hill.

If you want to go higher, you can go rock climbing like these people. They are brave and strong, but they don't want to fall.

Would you like to climb a mountain?

Mountains are very high!

You might meet with danger in some mountain paths, because of ice and snow.

Or there might be a big drop at the side of the path.

The tallest mountain on the planet is called **Mount Everest**.

To climb this mountain you would need the right equipment, boots and clothes.

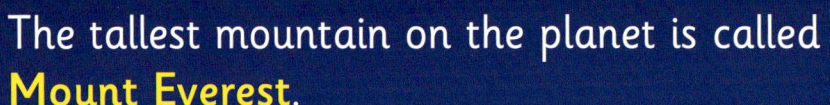

You would all fix **crampons** on the bottoms of boots to stop you slipping.

You might be roped to a second climber.

Mount Everest would take many days to climb. You would need to be very fit to attempt it!

Can you see these people climbing (or standing) on ladders? What are they all doing?

Where would you like to climb?